UNIVERSITY OF
GLOUCESTERSHIRE

at Cheltenham and Gloucester

Park Library
University of Gloucestershire
Park Campus, The Park, Cheltenham,
Gloucestershire GL50 2RH

This edition first published
in 2006
by UNIVERSE PUBLISHING
A division of Rizzoli
International Publications, Inc.
300 Park Avenue South
New York NY 10010
www.rizzoliusa.com

Copyright © 2006,
Marvin Scott Jarrett, Nylon LLC

Design by Michael Pangilinan
and Connie Makita

2006 2007 2008 2009
10 9 8 7 6 5 4 3 2

Printed in China

ISBN-10: 0-7893-1501-7
ISBN-13: 978-0-7893-1501-4
Library of Congress Control Number:
2006902122

PUBLISHER'S NOTE

Neither Universe
Publishing nor
NYLON has any
interest, financial
or personal, in
the businesses
listed in this
book. No fees
were paid or
services rendered
in exchange for
inclusion in these
pages.

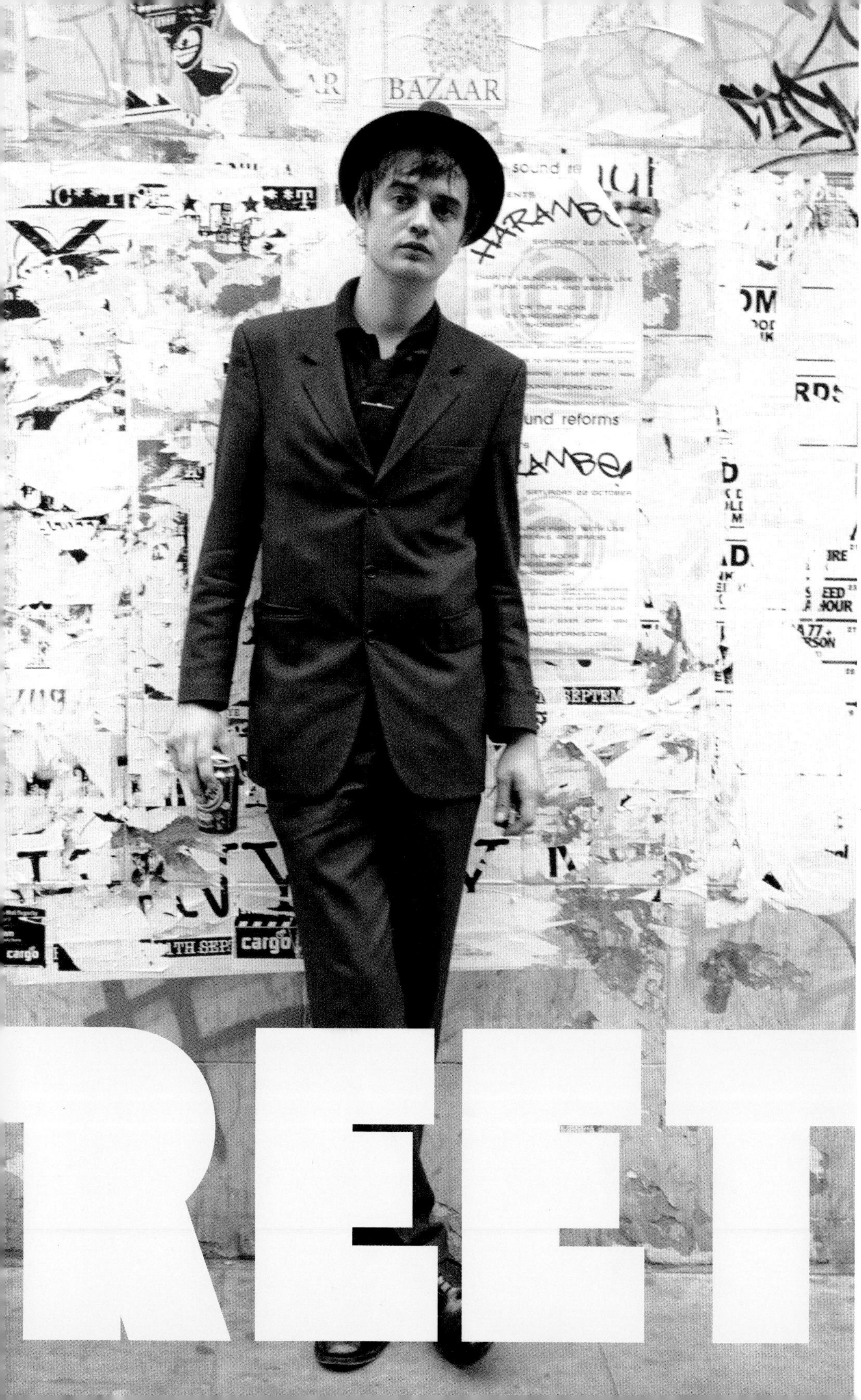

REET

Contents

FOREWORD

One of the best things about being the editor-in-chief of *NYLON* is the amount of travel it has allowed me to do. In the seven years since we founded the magazine out of a tiny room at The Standard in Hollywood, I've been to Berlin, Moscow, Tokyo, Rio, Sydney, Paris, London, Hong Kong—and that's just the beginning of the list. These trips have been inspiring to me not just because of the unique energy of the cities, but also because of the awesome style I've seen on their streets. Each place I've visited has a totally different look, and I've realized how much what people are wearing tells you about a city and its culture. The first time I went to Tokyo, for example, I was really surprised by the way certain tribes of kids would appropriate Western subcultures like British punk or rockabilly but turn them into totally new, over-the-top styles that you'd never see in this country. If Tokyo kids are dressing like they're going on stage, here in New York, where *NYLON* is based, everyone's dressing to get backstage. The idea is to impress the in-crowd, not every single passerby. But both of these cities, because of their unique local cultures, breed organic looks that thrive not on the catwalks but on the sidewalks. It was hard to narrow it down to seven cities for this book, but we ultimately decided that New York, London, Tokyo, Berlin, Paris, Melbourne, and Copenhagen are setting the pace for the rest of the world.

Another thing that I love about my job is that I can literally wear whatever I want to work—that goes for everyone at *NYLON*. People who know me definitely know that I have a fondness for jeans, hoodies, T-shirts, and sneakers (I have hundreds of pairs). It's not just stuff I happen to like; it says a lot about who I am. To us at *NYLON*, fashion is not what's in the stores on Madison Avenue, New Bond Street, or Omotesando Road, but what an individual mixes together to create a visible expression of their own personality. And as you'll see on the following pages, these kids have plenty of it.

Marvin Scott Jarrett
Editor-in-Chief, *NYLON*

INTRODU

If you want to see a fashion show, try sitting on the stoop outside the *NYLON* magazine loft in SoHo. On any given afternoon, you might encounter skateboarders whizzing by in limited-edition Nike Dunks; hip-hop kids in oversized hoodies; scruffy rockers in skinny jeans; fur-clad socialites; and fashionable strivers who pair brand-new designer dresssses with ratty vintage boots. Here in New York—as well as in other cultural capitals with a lot of people and not a lot of space—if you want to get somewhere, you'll probably walk. Urban life puts you on display for the world to see, and in that climate, how you dress speaks volumes about who you are—and who you'd like to be.

One of the major reasons *NYLON* launched in 1999 was because other magazines were missing an important point: Fashion doesn't exist in a bubble. To us, it's not only for rich people, models, and the type of people who slavishly adhere to runway trends; we see it as a living, breathing reflection of cultural and social currents, of what's going on in music, art, and on the sidewalks of the communities we live in. We celebrate this interaction each month in the pages of the magazine. As the ideas introduced on high-fashion runways become instantly accessible to the masses through the Internet and the recent phenomenon of "fast fashion" chain stores, everyone gets more daring. The messy, mixed-up

real-world results, in turn, influence what the industry produces. Trend-forecasting firms and mass-market retailers send teams to chase down what's happening on the street, while savvy designers and stylists simply know where to look. Take Marc Jacobs. Thanks to his Marc line, affluent suburban teens are dressing like Bushwick hipsters; thanks to his gig at Louis Vuitton, their mothers are carrying bags inspired by Harlem hip-hop. Style trickles up, not just down.

As the world gets smaller and cultures intermingle, options for personal expression multiply exponentially. Whereas city dwellers of past generations wore a uniform to school, and, once they got older, another kind of uniform to work, the notion of culturally mandated dress codes—in the West, at least—has disappeared as rapidly as the invisible lines that once divided races and social classes. Style, ultimately, is as much about the wearer as what is worn. And the social and cultural mobility afforded by the Internet means that people can,

CTION

through the use of clothing, invent themselves. We can dress in a way that proudly announces where we're from; we can declare our rebellion against it. We can announce that we belong to a subcultural group, or do our damnedest to cover it up. We can wear what we want, when we want, and if the photos in this book are any indication, what we're wearing is as fascinating as ever.

Street style photography may be a relatively recent phenomenon, but its roots are in the documentary tradition. The tribes of mid-century London were a favorite subject of David Bailey, and even earned their own serious exhibit at the Victoria and Albert Museum in 1995. Billy Name snapped the action at Warhol's factory; Jamel Shabazz did the same for New York's early hip-hop scene. London's *i-D* magazine documented the city's rebels and misfits and in the process changed the look of high-fashion photography. In Japan, where subcultures morph and mutate almost daily, young people race to outdo one another, hoping to be photographed for *FRUiTS* magazine; countless websites devote themselves to the topic. The subjects chosen for this book do not represent a random sample of young people in each city. Rather, we chose those with a certain something—a vibe, a way of putting things together—that transcends the manic blur of the city streets. These people, for one reason or another, made us look.

If we had our way, we'd hit every major city in the world in search of fash-

ion fresh from the streets, but space constraints forced us to choose just a few. Some were immediately obvious: New York, which needs no explanation; Tokyo, famous for its subcultural extremes, where savvy kids barely into their teens toy with notions of race and gender; London, where the original Mods and Teddy Boys defined the concept of street style decades ago, and a rock and grime underground now thrives; Berlin, where a new avant-garde has filled the vacuum created when the wall came down; and Paris, the undisputed capital of chic. In addition, we decided to visit two unexpected but undeniably stylish cities we feel are the next frontiers of sartorial innovation: Copenhagen, whose tradition of intelligent, modern design is now being echoed in a new wave of creativity; and, on the other side of the equator, Melbourne, Australia's "second city," which is second to none in its underground spirit and diversity. The unique combination of geographical and historical factors in these seven cities, along with their particular creative and cultural currents, give them a look all their own. Watch and learn.

PETER, 26
I'M WEARING an old suit—a fine cut
of cloth from Jeeves & Wooster's
I'VE BEEN LISTENING to Billie Holiday,
Wolfman, Blondie, and Motown greats
MY FAVORITE FASHION TREND
is braces (suspenders)
THE BEST THING ABOUT LONDON
is Arcady Dawn in Whitechapel

LONDON

There was a time when the sun never set on the British Empire, when London exerted an influence on global culture that will probably never be matched. Today, London remains one of the most international, if idiosyncratic, cities in the world. It's a curious, dichotomous mix of old (Tower of London, Houses of Parliament) and new (Piccadilly Circus, the London Eye) that offers tourists so many photo opportunities that few delve deep enough to experience the underside of what is a dynamic, cosmopolitan, and quintessentially alternative city. (Punk was born here, don't forget.) Contradictions abound at every step. There are reminders of royalty everywhere, yet it's the home of the second-oldest parliamentary democracy in the world (the first was Iceland). The City of London proper only covers an area of one square mile around the Bank of London, but the sprawling mess of overlapping boroughs and villages that has built up around it is one of the most diverse metropolises on earth. It's a place that is all about the parts off-center; the middle—from the bright lights of Leicester Square to the glittering monoliths of Buckingham Palace and St. James's Palace—is really only the beginning, a watered-down tourist dream of a city that, for all of its archaic traditions, buzzes with an alternative scene to rival the very best in the world.

In 1576, Shakespeare's first-ever theatre opened its doors just off Curtain Road, in the East End of London. At that time, the region was outside the city's walls; today it is an epicenter of vibrant music and fashion with a dynamic club scene. Prior to the 1980s, the grimy, red-bricked area—which now falls into the geographical jurisdiction of Shoreditch and Hoxton—was mostly printing and stock warehouses; after these businesses moved to the Docklands, it fell into disrepair. Then, in the early 1990s, the fashion and art crowds moved in. Central Saint Martins, one of the pre-eminent fashion colleges in the world, now has a campus on Curtain Road, and while a few asymmetrical haircuts and ripped jeans are not going to revive the adventurous spirit the area once had, there is still a lot to be said for some of the bars on and around Brick Lane, where people aren't afraid to get dressed up or throw a party.

Farther east still is the birthplace of London's now-infamous grot 'n' roll scene: The Rhythm Factory on Whitechapel Road sprang up around the Libertines but didn't dissipate when they did. Indeed, if the photography (and designs) of Hedi Slimane are anything to go by, the crowd here still wields a major influence over fashion. Also in the east, Hackney has experienced a major resurgence, as has Bethnal Green. Farther south, the squat scenes in Peckham and Dalston are gradually impinging on the underground art movement in London in their own unique way.

Central London shouldn't be totally overlooked, however. While a lot of people would dismiss Notting Hill on the grounds that it is too gentrified—or just plain boring—the tall white Victorian townhouses and trendy boutiques of the area are still offset by the ever-exciting Portobello Road market on the weekends, and some of the best vintage stores in the city. And the capital's central artery, Oxford Street, boasts arguably the most fashion-forward single store in the world: Topshop, the fast-fashion chain that gives back to its community by sponsoring (and hiring) the work of emerging local talent.

There are many who bemoan the glory days of London fashion, and who point to the fact that designers such as Stella McCartney, Alexander McQueen, and now even Brian Kirkby and Zowie Broach of Boudicca have turned their attention abroad as indicative of a falling international fashion profile. But, in reality, it's precisely the relocation of such internationally renowned names that makes London the most invigorating of all the fashion capitals. The McQueens and McCartneys have left behind a new generation of designers; anywhere else they might never get the opportunity to design their own lines. Preen, Bora Aksu, Miki Fukai, Richard Nicoll, Emma Cook, Jonathan Saunders, and Giles Deacon make London the most exciting, if commercially challenging, city on the Fashion Week circuit, and the city can also boast the industry's most innovative off-schedule program, On | Off, which corrals many of the city's fledgling talents into an interactive space at the Royal Academy. Inventive local streetwear labels like Maharishi and Silas have cult followings the world over. Oh, and Vivienne Westwood, one of the most influential designers in recent history, hasn't gone anywhere.

Westwood was the doyenne of the punk movement in the 1960s, and the city remains an unparalleled spawning ground of exhilarating music (electroclash, grime)—and fashion—subcultures. London kids dress to impress (and, often, to shock). Just as the city's catwalks challenge conventional notions of wearability, so too do the looks on the city's sidewalks. Here, exaggerated proportions and quirky colors are the norm. And while vintage dressing may be a relatively recent phenomenon elsewhere in the world, it's London that pioneered the concept. No one mixes oddball antique finds from Spitalfields Market with the latest Robert Cary-Williams for Topshop tunic or ratty old school sweaters with bondage pants from the Camden stables quite like Londoners. From a distance, the city's myriad style tribes may seem to blur into one amorphous, many-headed whole, but look more closely and its many pockets, from Brixton to Camden, each have a distinct individuality. You can't pin down a specific look for London, because it's a city defined by its very diversity.

MY FASHION ICON is Anaïs Nin

DIANA, 20

ROSANNA, 22
OCCUPATION fashion designer
I'M WEARING a jacket from my
own label, Rosanna Julie, and
everything else is secondhand
MY FAVORITE PIECE OF CLOTHING
is a really nice skirt with
pink poodles on it from Dolce
& Gabbana

DAVID, 25
OCCUPATION stylist
I'M WEARING '70s bohemia
MY FAVORITE FASHION TREND
is anything by Carol
Christian Poell
THE BEST THING ABOUT LONDON
is the chaos

I'M WEARING a jacket from Portobello
Market that didn't have a zip until I
found a perfect fit on an old coat in
a house I was renovating

MATT, 23, BUILDER

GABRIELLA, 19
OCCUPATION student
I'M WEARING self-made clothes
I'VE BEEN LISTENING TO Velvet
Underground, The Knife, Squeeze
MY FAVORITE FASHION TREND
is being out of style

ALXANDER, 15
I'VE BEEN LISTENING TO
The Cure, Pearl Jam, PJ Harvey,
Mr. Bungle
MY FAVORITE PIECES OF CLOTHING
are these sailor shoes
THE BEST THING ABOUT LONDON
is the youth

THE BEST THING ABOUT LONDON
is the architectural quality of
historical layering

EMILY, 21

I'M WEARING an outfit that's
kind of New Wave/Ramones
mixed with "I haven't washed
my clothes in ages"

GAVIN, 18

SAMUEL, 19
OCCUPATION musician
I'M WEARING dirt-cheap plimsolls
with ladies' jeans
MY FAVORITE PIECE OF CLOTHING
is a £5 Casio watch
MY FASHION ICONS ARE
The Fonz, Julian Casablancas,
and Ferris Bueller

SUSANNE, 24
OCCUPATION student
I'M WEARING what was lying on
my bedroom floor this morning
I'VE BEEN LISTENING TO
The Raveonettes, The Knife,
Depeche Mode, Eurythmics
THE BEST THING ABOUT LONDON
is the mixture of people from
all over the world

KANAKO, 21
OCCUPATION graphic design student
I'M WEARING Miss Sixty pants
and a top from Beyond Retro
MY FAVORITE PLACES TO SHOP
are the markets at Brick Lane
and Portobello Road
THE BEST THING ABOUT LONDON
is that there are a lot of
fashionable people

26

CARL, 24
OCCUPATION Musician
I'M WEARING black, because
it's the day before Halloween
I'VE BEEN LISTENING TO
Led Zeppelin
MY FAVORITE PIECE OF CLOTHING
is an old mohair jumper that
belonged to Sid Vicious
THE BEST THING ABOUT LONDON
is that it's 120 miles away from
the city I used to live in

MY FAVORITE PLACES TO SHOP
are trashy places like
Primark, where I buy kids'
clothes and remake them

BROOKE, 17

ALEX, 26
OCCUPATION shop assistant
I'M WEARING tight jeans
MY FAVORITE PLACES TO SHOP
are Rokit and Beyond Retro
MY FAVORITE FASHION TRENDS
are '80s and Japanese style
THE BEST THINGS ABOUT LONDON
are the fashion, and that
you can't get bored here

I'M WEARING a top I got for
one quid, a belt I stole
from my flatmate, and a bag
from the Fashion East party

DOMINIC, 20

YVONNE, 20
OCCUPATION painter/model
I'VE BEEN LISTENING TO
everything from old rock
to hip-hop
THE BEST THING ABOUT LONDON
is that even though I live a
busy lifestyle, I can
always find a quiet place

NANA, 32
OCCUPATION artist/illustrator
I'M WEARING what Jimi(ma) Hendrix
would be wearing in the present day
MY FAVORITE PLACE TO SHOP
is Euforia on Lancaster Road
I'VE BEEN LISTENING TO The Clash,
Toots & The Maytals, The Police,
The Smiths
MY FASHION ICON is Chryssie Hynde

MAEDA, 23
OCCUPATION art student
I'M WEARING '60s vintage shoes
from Camden and a '60s vintage
bag from Portobello
MY FASHION ICON is Pete Doherty
THE BEST THING ABOUT LONDON
is the indie rock scene

JULIAN, 23
OCCUPATION musician
I'VE BEEN LISTENING TO Orange
Juice, Dirty Three, Mystery Jets
MY FASHION ICON is Mick Jagger
THE BEST THING ABOUT LONDON
is Portobello Market

ALAN, 22
OCCUPATION actor/shop assistant
I'M WEARING an old cowboy shirt,
my Dad's T-shirt, an army
training T-shirt from the '70s,
Levi's, and Converse All Stars
MY FAVORITE FASHION TREND
is cowboy mixed with rock
THE BEST THINGS ABOUT LONDON
are the diversity of culture and
24-hour tobacco

MY FASHION ICON is Charlie Chaplin

MATT, 18

CARMEN, 22
I'M WEARING a vintage top and
denim shorts with a jacket
and boots from Euforia, where I work
MY FAVORITE PLACE TO SHOP
is the Camden stables
I'VE BEEN LISTENING TO
Animal Collective, Clap Your
Hands Say Yeah, Cat Power, and
the Duke Spirit

ADELE, 16
OCCUPATION student
I'M WEARING clothes I
found in my bag
I'VE BEEN LISTENING TO
Four Tet, Wet Dog, Blackwire
THE BEST THING ABOUT LONDON
is the men

PER, 18
OCCUPATION living and working
MY FAVORITE PLACES TO SHOP
are secondhand stores
I'VE BEEN LISTENING TO
Iggy Pop and the Smiths

I'M WEARING this because who
else do you see wearing it?
LUCY, 19

SERGIO, 24
OCCUPATION hairdresser
I'M WEARING what I woke up
and put on
I'VE BEEN LISTENING TO
Bauhaus, Depeche Mode, Antony
& The Johnsons
MY FAVORITE FASHION TREND
is GOTH!
MY FASHION ICON
is Marilyn Manson

MARIE, 23
OCCUPATION sales assistant
I'M WEARING a vintage coat
from the '60s
MY FAVORITE PLACE TO SHOP
is Brick Lane
I'VE BEEN LISTENING TO
Arcade Fire, Black Keys, The
Kinks, Bob Dylan, and The Clash

JAKOB, 25
OCCUPATION stylist
I'M WEARING secondhand hungover
I'VE BEEN LISTENING TO
Bowie, Kings of Leon, Kate Bush
THE BEST THING ABOUT LONDON
is its diversity

MY FAVORITE FASHION TRENDS
are oversized and quirky
PATHAMA, 19

WOMEN

FRED, 18
OCCUPATION Musician
I'VE BEEN LISTENING TO
Les Incompetents, Test Icicles,
Good Shoes, Best Fwends,
and Mystery Jets
MY FAVORITE FASHION TRENDS ARE
nu-gangsta/old-skool kool and
'80s hip-hop meets regal London
THE BEST THINGS ABOUT LONDON
are live music and tramps

ROB, 19
OCCUPATION actor
I'M WEARING the only things I've got
MY FASHION ICON IS James Dean

THE BEST THING ABOUT
LONDON is *not* the food

LOWE, 31

NUHA, 29
OCCUPATION artist
I'M WEARING what felt nice today
I'VE BEEN LISTENING TO
Babyshambles, Aphex Twin, Plaid,
The Killers
THE BEST THINGS ABOUT LONDON ARE
the Sunday markets and bagels on
Brick Lane

rtl

electri

Re:evaluate' out on

Herbe

Morell F

Bake

ns

CTOBER

Muck

Octo

LIVE

y

herlng

sonata

COPENHAGE

On the surface, Copenhagen looks almost too quaint to exist anywhere but in the pages of a fairy tale, far away from the twenty-first century world. Antique row houses and cobbled quays line its canals and harbors; delicate spires and ships' masts dot the sky. But hidden among the old-fashioned landmarks of Scandinavia's largest city is the shock of the new—from the high-tech driverless Metro system (built in 2002) to glassy new architectural experiments and the hip kids stomping the sidewalks.

Denmark has a long and illustrious creative tradition—among architecture buffs, the word "Danish" is essentially synonymous with "modern"—and in the past few years, droves of young Danes who might have otherwise sought fame and fortune in London or Paris have chosen to stay, albeit with a watchful eye toward what's going on in the rest of the world. Lars von Trier and his acolytes of the Dogme 95 filmmaking movement seized the international spotlight just over a decade ago; since then, local heroes the Raveonettes have helped form a respectable Copenhagen indie-rock scene. And a new, forward-thinking fashion underground is emerging, led by designers Henrik Vibskov, Wood Wood, Stine Goya, Baum und Pferdgarten; boutiques like 1206, Lola Pagola, Storm, and Nag; and magazines like *Dansk* and *Cover*. By the time the city decided to hold its first international fashion week in 2004, it was official: Something was in the air.

In the former red-light district of Vesterbro, just west of downtown, whorehouses are being reborn as rock clubs, meatpacking warehouses have mutated into exhibition spaces, and photographers and stylists live in row houses originally built for workers at the defunct Carlsberg brewery (itself now a pricey condominium). The Islands Brygge—once a wasteland of abandoned soybean silos—now teem with galleries and underground clubs. International bands fly in to play sold-out shows at Vega—a mid-century modern landmark structure that was formerly a meeting place for

THOMAS, 30
OCCUPATION
artist
I'VE BEEN
LISTENING to the
Beatles, Grand
Avenue, Motorhead,
Elvis Costello,
Led Zeppelin
MY FAVORITE PIECE
OF CLOTHING
is my dark blue
dinner jacket from
Dries Van Noten
THE BEST THINGS
ABOUT COPENHAGEN
are air, space,
and light

SOPHUS, 26
OCCUPATION
student at
the national
theater school
MY FASHION ICON
is Johnny Depp
in Cry-Baby

organized laborers—and in Christiania, a gated utopian commune where Danish drug laws don't apply. But in a city that's unusually compact and pedestrian-oriented, style is everywhere you go.

And as you'd expect in a country where babies are rocked to sleep in Arne Jacobsen chairs by the light of Verner Panton lamps, style is practically wired into the genetic code. Punk rock, 1980s-era New York, and the stark Hedi Slimane aesthetic are constant influences, as evidenced by the predominance of oversized hoodies, shaggy scarves, graphic prints, and tapered Acne jeans (all the better not to get stuck in your bike chain). But on the sidewalks of Copenhagen, even casual streetwear looks like something altogether more refined. Maybe it's because streamlined elegance is a national creed; maybe the largely purebred population, with its chiseled Nordic bone structure and long limbs, is simply better-looking than the rest of us. In any case, this tiny city packs an insane amount of style per square mile. See for yourself.

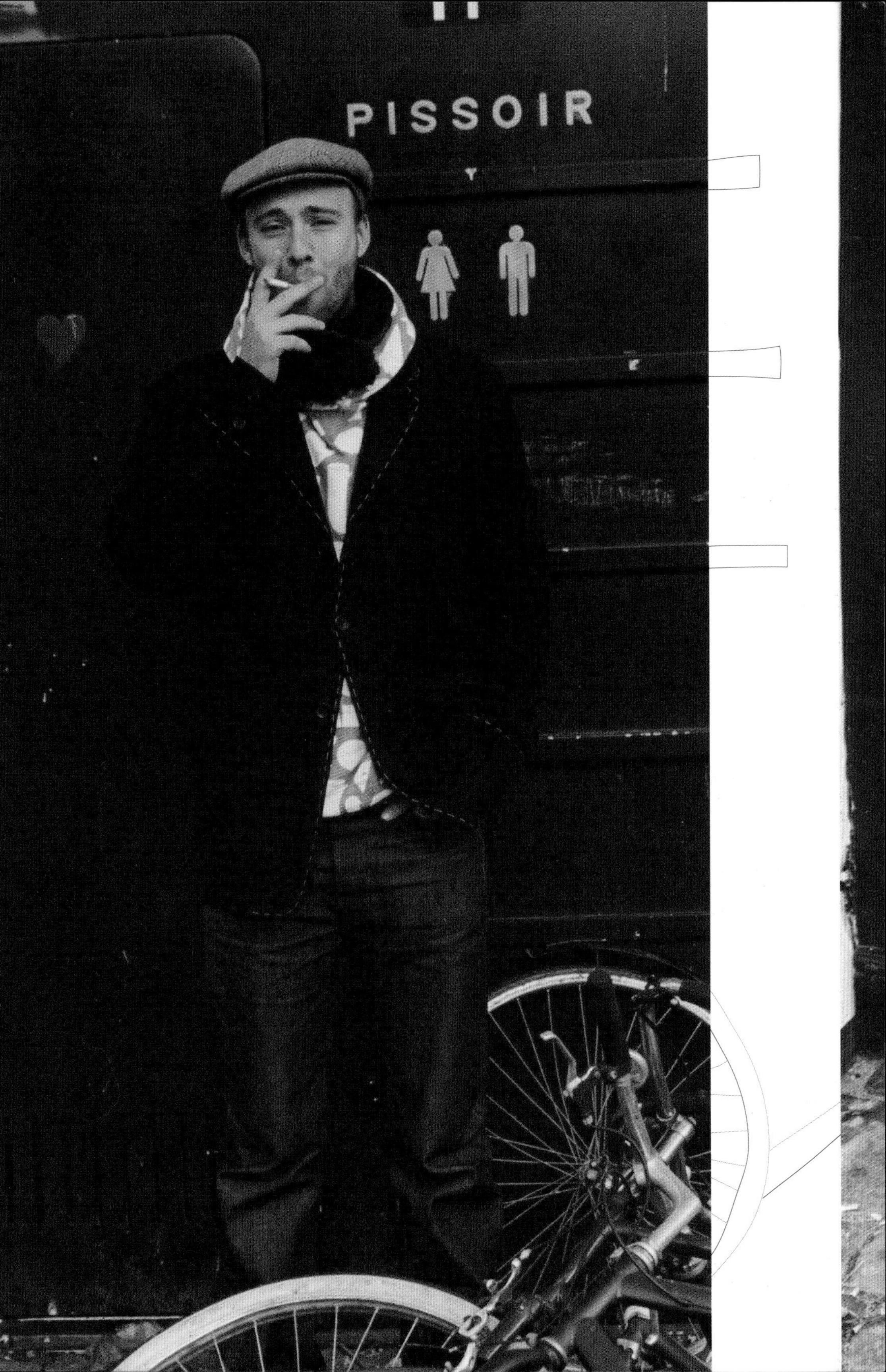
PISSOIR

MAGNUS, 26
OCCUPATION
manager/
co-founder of
Wood Wood
I'M WEARING
soft cloth
because it
feels nice
I'VE BEEN
LISTENING TO
Nick Drake,
Bob Dylan,
Public Enemy,
and Tommy Guerro

OLIVIA, 23
OCCUPATION
film and media
student/DJ
MY FAVORITE
PLACES TO SHOP
are obscure,
remote flea
markets or other
places untouched
by the evil hand
of fashion
THE BEST THINGS
ABOUT COPENHAGEN
are the late
summer's clear
blue sky and the
city swarmed with
beautiful women
in miniskirts
on bikes

RASMUS, 26
OCCUPATION
architect/bar
manager
MY FASHION ICON
is Christian
Benneweis
Hansen of LVMH
London

MY FAVORITE
FASHION TREND
is oversized
fanny packs
THE BEST THING
ABOUT COPENHAGEN
is rooftop
clubbing in the
summertime

BRIAN, 29
OCCUPATION
designer
I'M WEARING
New Balance
sneakers,
vintage Levi's
jeans, Rockwell
T-shirt, Lacoste
shirt, Silas
scarf
MY FAVORITE
PIECES OF
CLOTHING
are my Jordans
MY FAVORITE
FASHION TREND
is early-
'90s hip-hop
THE BEST THING
ABOUT COPENHAGEN
is the water

JOEKIM, 28
OCCUPATION
hair and makeup
artist
MY FAVORITE
PLACES TO SHOP
are 1206,
Naboles 3, Dede
and Stoffer
I'VE BEEN
LISTENING TO
Michael Mayer,
Kompact, Ferenc
Fraximal
MY FAVORITE
FASHION TREND
is the farmer
boy look

HELLE, 29
OCCUPATION
fashion designer/
illustrator
I'VE BEEN
LISTENING TO
The Knife, Wiley
MY FAVORITE
PLACES TO SHOP
are secondhand
stores and Wood
Wood
THE BEST THINGS
ABOUT COPENHAGEN
are my family
and friends

MY FASHION ICONS
are all the members
of my mom's old
ballet ensemble
JESPER, 22

KARL-OSKAR, 30
OCCUPATION
designer
I'VE BEEN
LISTENING TO the
Pixies, Wu-Tang
Clan, Megadeth,
Tommy Guerro
MY FAVORITE
PIECES
OF CLOTHING are
my collection of
Lacoste caps
THE BEST THING
ABOUT COPENHAGEN
is riding my
bike on cold
winter nights
when everybody
sleeps

JON, 26
OCCUPATION
fashion-related
multitasking
I'M WEARING one
half of a knit-
ted scarf made
by Bless because
it was too big
with both halves
MY FASHION ICON
is Henrik Vibskov

NANNA, 24
OCCUPATION
student/DJ
THE BEST
THING ABOUT
COPENHAGEN
is the smell
of the sea

MATHEW
ALBUM UDE NU!

MATHEW
ALBUM UDE NU!

MATHILDE, 23
OCCUPATION
model/psychology
student
I'M WEARING
a Hanes wife-
beater, Levi's
jeans, adidas
trainers, Ter et
Bantine jacket,
Paul Smith hat
THE BEST THINGS
ABOUT COPENHAGEN
are the light
and that you can
ride your bike
without having
to worry that
you might not
make it home

CHRIS, 28
OCCUPATION
fashion writer
I'M WEARING YSL
glasses, second-
hand jacket and
trousers, Acne
top, Helmut Lang
shoes, and an
Hermès belt, all
in black
MY FASHION
ICONS are Elvis
Costello and
Andy Warhol
THE BEST THING
ABOUT COPENHAGEN
is that it's in
the middle of a
major wave and
I'm surfing it

MY
FAVORITE
FASHION
TREND
is
techno-
hippie
LEVENT, 26

MAJA, 27
OCCUPATION
designer for
Henrik Vibskov
I'M WEARING
a Helle Mardahl
sweatshirt,
Cheap Monday
jeans, Vibskov
cape and scarf,
mens' leather
boots
THE BEST THING
ABOUT COPENHAGEN
is being able
to cycle

GYRITH, 20
OCCUPATION
student/editor
I'VE BEEN
LISTENING TO
Lali Puna,
Interpol,
Diefenbach
MY FAVORITE
PIECE OF
CLOTHING is my
slippers
THE BEST THING
ABOUT COPENHAGEN
is that it's
pretty close
to the rest of
the world

I'M WEARING
very old and
used All Stars,
Acne leather
pants, Marie
Seguy earrings,
and Marc Jacobs
sunglasses

METTE, 25

STINE, 26
OCCUPATION
designer
I'VE BEEN
LISTENING TO
Dolly Parton,
Interpol, Mew,
Flaming Lips
MY FAVORITE
PIECE OF CLOTHING
is a Jonathan
Saunders kimono
MY FASHION ICON
is some gay guy
from London
MY FAVORITE
FASHION TREND
is turbans

JESPER, 29
OCCUPATION
gallerist/art
director/DJ
I'M WEARING
my fall rock 'n'
roll wardrobe:
black Vans,
Levi's, Surface
2 Air T-shirts,
Army scarf, lum-
berjack jacket
MY FASHION ICON
is Kurt Cobain
THE BEST THING
ABOUT COPENHAGEN
is the freedom

MIKKEL, 24
OCCUPATION
goldsmith
MY FAVORITE
PLACE TO SHOP
is in a
bookstore
I'VE BEEN
LISTENING TO
Keren Ann,
Malcolm McLaren,
Annie Lennox,
Kraftwerk
THE BEST THING
ABOUT COPENHAGEN
is the
familiarness

ABSALON, 22
OCCUPATION
photographer's
assistant
MY FAVORITE
PLACE TO SHOP
is Netto
I'VE BEEN
LISTENING TO
Postal Service,
Kanye West
THE BEST THING
ABOUT COPENHAGEN
is that you can
smoke in bars

KASPER, 31
OCCUPATION
artist
I'VE BEEN
LISTENING TO
Antony and the
Johnsons, Rufus
Wainwright,
The Blackheart
Procession,
Fleetwood Mac,
Devendra
Banhart
MY FASHION ICON
is myself

MY
FASHION
ICON
is
Grace
Jones
SASSIE, 29

HENRIK, 33
OCCUPATION
designer
I'VE BEEN
LISTENING TO
Crystal Waters,
Radiohead, PJ
Harvey, Múm, Mew
MY FAVORITE
FASHION TREND
is socks. I'm very
keen on socks at
the moment
THE BEST THING
ABOUT COPENHAGEN
is my little boat

November 9, 1989. Mobs of East Berliners, emboldened by a premature announcement that they would be allowed to freely cross into West Berlin, showed up at the massive slab of concrete dividing the Communist-controlled half of the city from its capitalist counterpart. Overpowering the few unprepared guards on patrol, they streamed into West Berlin by the thousands, embracing their estranged compatriots and dancing in the streets. As the wall was chipped away by celebratory sledgehammers, a dark era of German history disintegrated with it.

During the decade that followed, a transformation on a scale unprecedented in modern culture took place. The formerly dreary, down-and-out precincts of East Berlin suddenly became a place where young Germans—and adventurous young people from all over Europe and the rest of the world—could live affordably. Artists, musicians, and designers in need of cheap studio space—plus sundry misfits and the merely curious—flocked to the east-central Mitte and Prenzlauer Berg neighborhoods, intrigued by the idea of creating a bohemia. Recently vacated GDR government buildings were commandeered by enterprising new residents and transformed into illegal speakeasies and techno clubs—until the police shut them down and they moved on to the next space. Renegade galleries sprung up. Graffiti bloomed. The Kunst-Werke, Berlin's center for contemporary art, was founded in 1990 when a group of young art lovers colonized a Mitte margarine factory. And a little get-together called Love Parade organized a few months before the fall of the wall, grew over the course of the 1990s into the largest techno-music festival in the world, with millions of attendees flying in to celebrate dancing, sex, mind-altering substances, and mind-altering fashion. Word spread to London, Paris, Tokyo, and New York: Berlin was the place to be.

The result of this mass creative migration is a thriving, if still undefined, scene in Berlin today. The musical genre known as electroclash—following in the footsteps

of the Düsseldorf electronic pioneers Kraftwerk and Neu! from the 1970s and 1980s—was born at back-alley performances of glam artists like Chicks on Speed, Peaches, and Cobra Killer. Kitty Yo Records and DJ Ellen Allien's BPitch Control label support albums of electronic artists from around the world, as do Berlin's legendary all-night dance clubs. Artwise, the city has emerged as Europe's most prolific production center, as creative types from the continent and farther afield flock to the still-inexpensive city to work and live among the like-minded. Wealthy collectors from London and Cologne prowl the galleries around Auguststrasse in Mitte, or near Checkpoint Charlie in West Berlin's Kreuzberg, in hopes of discovering the next big thing. Mitte, Prenzlauer Berg, and Kreuzberg have matured into destinations for upwardly mobile media types and the advertising agencies and publishing houses that employ them, while more adventurous (or more broke) bohemian types branch farther out to neighborhoods of Friedrichshain and, increasingly, Wedding.

Meanwhile, the city has developed a fashion-forward sensibility that is uniquely its own. While many of Berlin's high-end boutiques can be found in the more bourgeois western borough of Charlottenburg, it's in Mitte where the fashion pulse of the city truly beats. There, you'll find Bless, a design collective that blurs the lines between art and fashion; Apartment, a clandestine subterranean space famed for spearheading Berlin's shopping renaissance; and Andreas Murkudis, who sells wares from Europe's most adventurous designers, including his brother Kostas. To see how it all gets put together, stroll down café- and shop-lined Kastanienallee in Prenzlauer Berg. Sleek streetwear is mixed with 1980s vintage, seasoned with a dash of graphic extremism—a jet-black bowl cut here, jet-black eyeliner there—that somehow seems appropriate among the city's foreboding mix of Gothic and modern architecture. The culture of intellectual curiosity, the clash between old and new, extends to the culture of dressing.

This is, after all, the city where Mies van der Rohe's Bauhaus changed the course of design; this is where Rei Kawakubo of Comme des Garçons chose to set up her first guerrilla store; this is where the cerebral designs of C-Neeon and Miroïke—some of the international fashion scene's brightest new stars—are conceived. Even though the city's (and country's) economic status is still shaky, Berlin remains a field of dreams, a sort of anti-Hollywood for the avant-garde. Most of the people photographed in this chapter were children at the time the wall fell; the event made an indelible impression. However uncertain Berlin's identity and fate, a belief in the power of creativity—and a sense of hopefulness—prevails. You can see it on their faces.

KATHARINA, 24

OCCUPATION Student I'M WEARING clothes covered with skulls because I'm feeling good in them I'VE BEEN LISTENING TO A Thousand Falling Skies, On Broken Wings, Aiden MY FAVORITE FASHION TRENDS are punk and rockabilly

THE BEST THING ABOUT BERLIN is that sometimes very, very special things happen here KATARZYNA, 22

KWESI, 29
OCCUPATION Musician I'M WEARING this outfit to feel cool MY FASHION ICON is Isaac Hayes
THE BEST THINGS ABOUT BERLIN are my friends, the parks, and the parties

KAROLINE, 24
OCCUPATION Actress I'VE BEEN LISTENING TO the Garden State soundtrack and Cocorosie
MY FASHION ICON is Sienna Miller THE BEST THINGS ABOUT BERLIN are Oderberger Strasse and the aquarium

MARIE-CECILE, 22
OCCUPATION Fashion student I'M WEARING a mix of things, including a pair of silk pants from my last collection
THE BEST THINGS ABOUT BERLIN ARE the people I like, vast apartments, and the many reasons for getting drunk

EIKE, 18

THE BEST THINGS ABOUT BERLIN are Stabi West, Tiergarten, and Prateo

JO, "born in the last century"
OCCUPATION Fashion designer I'M WEARING a Margiela pullover, a shawl by Phriedjung, vintage Levi's, vintage boots, and a belt from a Turkish market, because everything else was dirty MY FASHION ICON IS no one else but me THE BEST THINGS ABOUT BERLIN ARE the club culture, the TV tower, and my Plattenbau apartment

LINDA, 20
OCCUPATION Fashion student MY FAVORITE PLACES TO SHOP are Harajuku in Tokyo and Camden in London MY FAVORITE PIECES OF CLOTHING are a jacket and skirt by Baby the Stars Shine Bright I'VE BEEN LISTENING TO Gwen Stefani, Gackt, Moi Dix Mois, Ayumi Hamasaki

THE BEST THINGS ABOUT BERLIN are the freedom, creativity, and cheap prices

JAN, 23

HE-JI
I'M WEARING nothing much MY FASHION ICON IS Yoko Ono THE BEST THINGS ABOUT BERLIN ARE the people and the streets

CLAUDE, 23
OCCUPATION singer/performer in LoveLoveLove I'M WEARING an outfit by LoveLoveLove and jewelry by Lucy Bukovsky, because I lovelovelove it MY FASHION ICONS ARE Lucy Bukovsky and Issey Miyake THE BEST THINGS ABOUT BERLIN ARE the freedom, space, time, and creativity

JAN, 23

OCCUPATION student I'M WEARING a Costume National jacket, Dsquared2 shirt, Evisu pants, and Dior Homme shoes
MY FASHION ICON is me THE BEST THINGS ABOUT BERLIN are the clubs, the people, and the bars

MARKUS
I'M WEARING Emerica pants, Vans, and a vintage leather jacket MY FASHION ICONS ARE Hedi Slimane and Pete Doherty
THE BEST THING ABOUT BERLIN IS the long parties

MARIA, 22

OCCUPATION Art student I'M WEARING a vintage dress and boots MY FAVORITE PLACES TO SHOP ARE Kleidermarkt and Garage at Nollendorfplatz I'VE BEEN LISTENING TO Nouvelle Vague, Blondie, Le Tigre

PABLO, 23

OCCUPATION artist I'M WEARING Kung fu sneakers and a Karl Lagerfeld for H&M jacket MY FASHION ICON is Tom Sawyer THE BEST THING ABOUT BERLIN is that every human emotion finds a place to be expressed

MIRJAM, 25

OCCUPATION Student I'M WEARING the best outfit I have MY FASHION ICON is my friend Katharina

THE BEST THING ABOUT BERLIN is the freedom you can feel here—it's spacious, green, and dirty

PARIS

Wherever the parameters of the fashion world are, Paris is its capital. The prevailing arbiter of sartorial elegance since the Renaissance, the city has been home to the fashion houses of Charles Frederick Worth (the first fashion designer to transcend the job title "dressmaker"), Elsa Schiaparelli, Christian Lacroix, Lucien Lelong, Jeanne Lanvin, Cristobal Balenciaga, Yves Saint Laurent, and Christian Dior, among many, many others. In 1854, a young man named Louis Vuitton began manufacturing trunks in the city; in 1921, the first bottle of Chanel No. 5 (the first fragrance to be specifically created by a fashion house) went on sale there; in the fall of 2005, American ex-pat Marc Jacobs, the man who turned Vuitton into a global megabrand, opened a suitably massive new flagship store on the Champs-Elysées complete

with a live Vanessa Beecroft installation of naked models. But beneath (and often alongside) the city's baroque, expensive, and highly polished veneer lies an altogether different kind of culture.

In September 2004, Parisian police discovered a fully equipped cinema-cum-restaurant in a skull-lined subterranean cavern deep beneath the stately sixteenth arrondissement. At first, authorities didn't know what to think. Was it a nesting ground for terrorists? A ritual center for satanists? A week later, it was revealed to be the meeting place of La Mexicaine de la Perforation, a clandestine circle of "urban explorers" whose mission was "to reclaim and transform disused city spaces for the creation of zones of expression for free and independent art." As their leader noted in an interview, about ten other groups were doing the same thing. And they always seemed to be one step ahead of getting caught. While not all of Paris's cultural innovators are quite so literally underground, the tale is a fitting metaphor for the almost shocking proximity between tradition and rebellion in this most traditional of cities.

CAROLINE, 22
OCCUPATION
model
I'M WEARING an imitation Dior sweater from Topshop in London and a leather jacket from Zara
I'VE BEEN LISTENING TO Madonna's *Confessions on a Dance Floor*
MY FAVORITE FASHION TRENDS are the Twiggy look, military, and girly-sexy à la Chloé

ALICE, 22
OCCUPATION
model
I'M WEARING
a marine jacket
with jeans, a
T-shirt, and a
bag from H&M
MY FASHION ICON
is no one in
particular;
I take inspi-
ration from
the shows and
magazines
THE BEST THINGS
ABOUT PARIS
are Jean Roch's
V.I.P. room on
the Champs-
Elysées and
pain au chocolat

VALENTIN, 28
OCCUPATION
photographer
I'VE BEEN
LISTENING TO
the Yeah Yeah
Yeahs and
Benny Benassi
THE BEST THINGS
ABOUT PARIS
are the aerial
subway line dur-
ing the night,
the French bad
boys called the
"Racailles," and
the bourgeoises
girls

Take the Palais de Tokyo. Standing on the broad Avenue du Président Wilson in the sixteenth, just across the Seine from the Eiffel Tower, the massive neoclassical exhibition space, built in 1937 and unused for years, was reopened in 2002 as a contemporary art center with exhibitions open until midnight. Wander inside on a Saturday night, and the wildly styled crowd at the bar—everyone who's anyone in the music and art worlds—should put to rest any doubts about the existence of a Paris avant-garde. Even the gift shop—owned by local graffiti guru André—is a 7-Eleven–style convenience store stocking art objects, Japanese toys, and outré clothing.

As the city's architecture and infrastructure evolve, the old stereotypes of the Rive Gauche (the bohemian Left Bank) and Rive Droite (the more traditional Right Bank) seem increasingly outmoded. Paris is a relatively small city, and while some neighborhoods are more lively than others—namely, the Marais, home to the Centre Pompidou, many of the city's fashion showrooms and independent boutiques, and, yes, tourists—there is no single place to be. Hipsters are spreading north and west to Bastille, Oberkampf, Belleville, and Pigalle, but they're just as likely to haunt basement bars in the gentrified Saint-Germain-des-Prés, or dance until dawn at Maxim's, Le Baron, and Le Paris Paris, some of the city's best clubs, which happen to be located in the quiet eighth and first arrondissements. (As Daft Punk, Alan Braxe, and Air will attest, Paris is one of the world's foremost producers of electronic music.)

While the city's social scene has gotten more interesting, so has its sense of style. Though the big guns—Chanel, Vuitton, YSL, Lanvin, Balenciaga, et al—continue to influence fashion on both a local and international scale, they're not the only game in town. Newer, archetypically French brands like A.P.C., Vanessa Bruno, and the

music-clothing collective Kitsune infuse everyday basics with an unmistakable elegance. Young designers like Nicholas Andreas Taralis, Charles Anastase, and Mélodie Wolf are offering graphically adventurous new takes on what French fashion can mean. And ever-inventive Parisians are mixing it all with handicrafts from the city's immigrant enclaves or budget buys from Guerrisol (Paris's counterpart to the Salvation Army). Colette, the cutting-edge emporium on the posh rue Saint-Honoré, made waves in 1997 by being the first "lifestyle" store to sell art books, graffiti-wrapped candy, gourmet meals, mix CDs, and gadgets; now every international city has a clone. And even the fabled haute couture shows are usually crashed by an upstart-designer prankster or two.

In Paris, dressing well and looking chic isn't antithetical to being cool; it's a way of life. In no other place will you find so many girls sporting prim trench coats and Chanel bags—the ultimate symbols of bourgeois correctness—with choppy haircuts and edgy eye makeup. Paris is where the neck scarf—Catherine Deneuve's favorite fashion trick—never fails to seem fresh. It's where guys can rock oversized hoodies and still somehow look gentlemanly. The tension between stubbornly enduring national heritage and urban modernity yields a culture—and, as the photos in this chapter make plain, a sense of style—unlike that of any other city. Paris's new identity is emerging not in spite of its traditions, but because of them.

TOMMY, 22
OCCUPATION
folk singer
I'M WEARING
the traditional
gown of my
tribe's leader
on the day of
sacrifice
THE BEST THING
ABOUT PARIS
is when the
bricks turn from
green to red in
the fall

MY FASHION
ICON is
my grand-
mother,
who never
gets tired
of wearing
clogs!
LINDA, 25

THE BEST
THINGS ABOUT
PARIS are the
everyday
markets, its
culture, the
piano concerts
in the St. Ju-
lian le Pauvre
Church, and
the coffee and
cigarettes
and flowers
and *chocolat
chaud* in the
St. Germain
des Prés

ALZBETA, 22

SIMON, 22
OCCUPATION
filmmaking
I'M WEARING
an aNYthing
T-shirt, an
A.P.C. jacket,
Nike shoes,
Agnès b. pants
I'VE BEEN
LISTENING TO
Queens of the
Stone Age and
bluegrass
MY FAVORITE
PLACE TO SHOP
is A.P.C.
THE BEST THINGS
ABOUT PARIS
are the movie
theaters and
buildings

MÉLANIE, 26
OCCUPATION
photographer
MY FASHIONS ICON
are Karen O,
David Bowie, and
Lydia Lunch
THE BEST THINGS
ABOUT PARIS
are taking
a coffee for
hours, and
smoking
cigarettes
everywhere

MY FASHION
ICONS are
Bettie Page
and Marilyn
Monroe
SANDRA, 22

GABE, 28
OCCUPATION
bass player
I'M WEARING
an old T-shirt,
shiny trousers
and big boots
from Dior Homme,
and a vintage
white belt from
eBay because
it's all I've got
MY STYLE ICON
is Witold
Gombrowicz for
understated
arrogance
THE BEST THING
ABOUT PARIS
is the sunset
on the Rue de
Sèvres

ANTONIA, 24

OCCUPATION
seller at
A.P.C.

I'M WEARING
A.P.C. jeans
and sweater,
a beret from
Sonia Rykiel,
a vintage
leather
jacket, and
Repetto shoes

I'VE BEEN
LISTENING TO
Sonic Youth,
the Rolling
Stones

MY FASHION
ICONS are
Liv Ullmann,
Juergen Teller,
and Sigourney
Weaver

PACOME
(too sleepy
to answer)

JACQUES, 25
OCCUPATION
life enjoyer
I'M WEARING
a kimono shirt
by Gucci, a
military
embroidered
jacket by Dior
Homme, jeans by
Yves Saint Lau-
rent, and sneak-
ers by adidas
MY FASHION ICONS
are anyone or
anything whose
image makes me
feel desire
THE BEST THINGS
ABOUT PARIS are
the cafés, where
you can spend
hours and hours,
the Left Bank,
the glamour, the
architecture

ANTONIA, 25
OCCUPATION
student at the
Sorbonne
I'M WEARING
all vintage
with an
Isabel Marant
dress worn
as a scarf
MY FASHION ICON
is designer
Lovisa Burfitt,
because she's
purrfect
THE BEST THINGS
ABOUT PARIS
are raindrops
on roses
and whiskers
on kittens

SHINA, 29
OCCUPATION
art director
I'M WEARING
boots by Sport-
max, customized Levis,
a T-shirt a
friend brought
me from Thai-
land, a Topshop
suit jacket,
a Balenciaga
jacket, a vin-
tage bag, and
earrings some
hippies in
Brazil gave
to me
I'VE BEEN
LISTENING TO
Bonnie "Prince"
Billy, Herman
Dune, The
Rapture, Cut
Copy, The Kills,
The Knife
THE BEST THINGS
ABOUT PARIS
are that you
find yourself
in film-like
situations all
the time, and
I never get
sick of the
Eiffel tower

THERESE, 20
I'M WEARING a
vintage jacket,
a Russian scarf,
a Comptoir des
Cotonniers car-
digan, double
layers of black
T-shirts, and
Acne jeans be-
cause I'm ill
today and I want
to be warm and
comfortable
MY FASHION ICONS
are the streets,
my friends,
and the time I'm
living in

EMILIE, 26
OCCUPATION
stylist's
assistant
I'M WEARING
a jacket and
jeans by Nicolas
Andreas Taralis,
vintage boots
and cardigan
MY FASHION ICON
is Serge
Gainsbourg
THE BEST THINGS
ABOUT PARIS
are the
cultural
inheritance,
quais de
la Seine,
and gardens

HITOMI, 29
OCCUPATION
stylist
I'M WEARING a
Marjan Pejoski
skirt, vintage
jacket, jumper,
bag, and boots
THE BEST THINGS
ABOUT PARIS
are the parks
and Canal
St. Martin

CÉLINE, 27
OCCUPATION
student
I'M WEARING
all vintage
MY FASHION ICON
is Jane Birkin
because she's so
beautiful even if
she's getting old

ALEXANDRE, 27
OCCUPATION
guitarist/
singer
I'M WEARING
vintage shoes,
ski socks,
very old Helmut
Lang jeans and
blouse, Zucca
T-shirt, Comme
des Garçons
belt and Xavier
Delcour belt
MY FASHION ICON
is Howard
Hughes because
he reminds me
of my father
THE BEST THINGS
ABOUT PARIS
are its École
des Beaux-Arts
and the strang-
ers I met there

MY FASHION ICON
is either Serge
Gainsbourg or Bob
Dylan because even
though they change
their clothes, the
clothes they wear
still keep a soul

EDVARD, 22

MIMI, 30
OCCUPATION
journalist/
agitator
I'M WEARING
a Preen jack-
et, a homemade
T-shirt, Chloé
jeans, retro
Italian pimp
shoes, and
a Celine bag
THE BEST
THINGS ABOUT
PARIS are the
culture, my
gorgeous
friends, and
goat cheese

LOVISA, 32
OCCUPATION
designer/
illustrator
MY FAVORITE
PLACE TO SHOP
is Onward
I'VE BEEN
LISTENING TO
the Rolling
Stones, The
White Stripes,
Patti Smith,
Mazzy Star
MY FASHION ICON
is Frida Kahlo;
she's the queen
THE BEST THINGS
ABOUT PARIS
are that it is
pretty, romantic
and magical; a
big city with a
warm soul

THE BEST THING
ABOUT PARIS
is that you
can walk from
one end of the
city to the
other in about
two hours,
and you'll
find everything
you want

AUDREY, 23

PERSEPHONE, 24
OCCUPATION
photographer
I'M WEARING
a Charles
Anastase jacket,
a vintage Celine
shirt, Zara
pants, Repetto
ballerina shoes
MY FAVORITE
PLACE TO SHOP
is a secondhand
shop in Paris
on the Rue de
Crussol
THE BEST THINGS
ABOUT PARIS
are that you eat
well and you
always see
someone you know
on the street

VALERIE, 23
OCCUPATION
student
I'M WEARING
wearing an old
vintage coat
MY FASHION ICON
is Grace Jones
because of
her androgyny

The best
things about
Paris
are the
Swedish folks,
taking a book
to the Jardin
des Tuileries,
and the
architecture

MIKA, 23

VALESKA, 25
OCCUPATION
assistant
stylist at
Chloé
I'M WEARING
a vintage
dress, Prada
shoes, and a
bag by Chloé
MY FASHION
ICONS are Karl
Lagerfeld and
Jane Birkin
THE BEST THINGS
ABOUT PARIS
are the lovely
new people that
I meet here
at the Sunday
markets

STÉPHANIE, 21
OCCUPATION
model
I'M WEARING
a Mango jacket,
a Japanese
pullover, Miss
Sixty jeans,
vintage boots
THE BEST THINGS
ABOUT PARIS
are the restau-
rants and my
friends

MY
FAVORITE
FASHION
TREND
is the
pajama
look
TWO TOM, 29

ELLEN, 25
OCCUPATION
stylist
I'M WEARING
Ann-Sofie Back,
Prada, Rodebjer,
Acne
MY STYLE ICON
is Maya Deren
THE BEST THINGS
ABOUT PARIS
are my friends
and the fashion

CHUCK, 29
OCCUPATION
I co-own THECAST,
a clothing company
I'M WEARING
black shoes and
jeans, a Brendan
Donnelly T-shirt,
a Plastic People
zip-up hoodie,
and no underwear

NEW

Eight million people and counting. Five boroughs. Is it possible that the whole world can exist within one city? It sure seems to in *NYLON*'s hometown, an ever-evolving metropolis that is the cultural capital of the United States and, in many ways, the world. Cultures, decades, and social currents converge like cars in a crosstown traffic jam: Punks, old-timers, nuevas latinas, electroclash trash, skate rats, art brats. It's all here, and we couldn't fully sum up its essence if we tried.

As the saying goes, geography is destiny, and nowhere is that more true than in the neighborhoods of New York. A couple of decades ago, young arrivals to the city might not think to live below Houston Street or east of Second Avenue—never mind across the East River. Now, neighborhoods downtown and in Brooklyn are the city's creative core. It started when post-industrial SoHo (South of Houston) was colonized by artists and gallerists in the 1970s. Over time, it became the world's most concentrated shopping mecca, home to every major designer in the world, as well as local institutions for fledgling talent like emerging-designer boutique Opening Ceremony and the Deitch Projects gallery. In recent years, artists and the young people who follow in their wake have spread across the southern reaches of the city, into the very neighborhoods their immigrant ancestors dreamed of escaping. Post-industrial TriBeCa, the quaint West Village, and formerly Italian NoLita are the most sought-after (and priciest) neighborhoods in the city. The East Village, birthplace of the Ramones and the Velvet Underground, still vibrates with rebellious energy thanks to the presence of NYU and an endless supply of bars and cafés. A few blocks south, on the Lower East Side's narrow Ludlow, Stanton, and Rivington streets, vintage shops and secret sneaker shrines are nestled next to Dominican hair salons and dive bars. Photographers, designers, and post-college types squeeze into the

YORK

same tenements their grandparents and great-grandparents once did. Walk past a metal trap door, and you'll probably hear a band practicing in the basement, perhaps in hopes of landing a gig at local upstart venues like Rothko, Cake Shop, and Pianos, or established ones like the Mercury Lounge and Tonic.

The other big story in New York in recent years has been the rebirth of Brooklyn. Across the East River, the grittily industrial neighborhood of Williamsburg has transformed from a rough, affordable artist enclave into a post-collegiate playground, thanks to music venues like Northsix and Warsaw, performance spaces like Galapagos, and more galleries than anywhere else in the city—except for West Chelsea, another neighborhood that has received an infusion of new blood as well as big money. Gentrification is sweeping eastward, through Puerto Rican enclaves and gutted-out Bushwick, and northward into previously predominantly Polish Greenpoint. Every morning, the L train is jammed with young people whose greatest creation so far is their own image: Dandies, tattooed metalheads, and girls who might have stepped out of the 1980s with their bowl cuts and vintage boots. There are so many of them, in fact, that the long-entrenched Hasidic community published a flyer calling for action against the "Plague of the Artists." On the other side of the old Brooklyn Navy Yard (now evolving into a furniture-design center and film studio) are the funky-yet-leafy brownstone neighborhoods of Boerum Hill, Clinton Hill, Fort Greene, Carroll Gardens, and Park Slope—along with the not-so-leafy former shipping enclave of Red Hook—where young creative types go for some peace and quiet. (Or, in the case of the newer performance venues springing up like Southpaw and The Hook, anything but.)

But if New York only had hipsters, it wouldn't be New York. Stroll down 125th Street in newly revived Harlem, or go to the South Bronx or the Fulton Mall in Downtown Brooklyn—the birthplaces of sneaker culture, famously documented by Jamel Shabazz in *Back in the Days*—and you'll see a multiethnic streetwise look all its own. Or hop the 7 train through Queens, and just try and count the number of languages you hear. Hit West Chelsea by day, when artists and gallerists dressed in Comme des Garçons and thick black glasses roam the streets. Or come back at night, when giant clubs spill over with wildly costumed crowds of people who've come from around the world to experience the legendary nightlife.

Where there's street life there's street style, and New York has both in spades. The collision of cultures and tastes on every block has a way of influencing the way people dress; New Yorkers love to play with references (ghetto-fab gold jewelry, rural Americana). On the other hand, there's also something very specific about New York—the extreme weather, the tough mindset, the constant movement that requires versatile clothes—that has continually produced fashion stars who define, and are defined by, what's come to be known as the "urban" look: Daryl K, whose rough-edged rocker aesthetic has stood the test of time and trends, creative streetwear companies like Nom de Guerre and Surface 2 Air, and citi-fied skate labels like Supreme. So what is the New York look, if there is one at all? The answer is as enigmatic as the city itself. People here like to say "once a New Yorker, always a New Yorker," and they've got a point: Whether Bronx-born and raised, transplanted Iowans, French ex-pats, or Asian-Americans, New Yorkers may resemble the rest of the world physically—but there's something about their style and attitude that you won't find anywhere else.

JESSIE, 27
OCCUPATION
dancer/musician
I'M WEARING
a jacket by Jen-
ny, a sweater by
Aaron, a skirt
by Gia, tights
by Mom, boots
by Olivia, and a
scarf by Emily
I'VE BEEN
LISTENING TO
Ghostface
Killah, Rub 'n'
Tug, Blue Label,
Shark Attack,
Apeshit
THE BEST THING
ABOUT NEW YORK
is playing bass
and singing
in Blue Label

PLEASE
NO VENDORS
HERE TO CURB

JAYMIE, 23
OCCUPATION
umm...
I'M WEARING
a Do Kham coat,
Tsubi jeans
that I had
tailored, and
a sweater
I squirreled
yesterday
MY FAVORITE
PLACE TO SHOP
is Narnia on
Rivington Street
I'VE BEEN
LISTENING TO
metal/pop/
audiobooks/Patti
Smith/Elvis
MY FASHION ICON
is Audrey
Hepburn

THE BEST
THING
ABOUT NEW
YORK is
that you
can have
what you
want when
you want it
TELFAR, 20

KENZO, 31
OCCUPATION
artist/designer
I'M WEARING
shiny, 'cos I'm
feeling shiny
MY FASHION ICON
is Michael Caine
THE BEST THING
ABOUT NEW YORK
is good coffee

MAY, 28
OCCUPATION
stylist
I'M WEARING
a flasher trench
coat with snake-
skin boots
MY FAVORITE PLACE
TO SHOP is eBay
MY FAVORITE PIECE
OF CLOTHING
is my bear/cat me-
dallion necklace
THE BEST THING
ABOUT NEW YORK is
being anonymous in
a crowd

KAZUSA
OCCUPATION
owner of Lovely
Day café on
Elizabeth Street
I'M WEARING
a vintage dress
and boots from
Eleven and
a Marc Jacobs
jacket
MY FAVORITE
PLACES TO SHOP
are Eleven and
eBay
I'VE BEEN
LISTENING TO
Jack White
bluegrass, Billy
Bragg, Crazy
Horse, Love,
Margo Guryan,
The The
MY FASHION ICON
is Marianne
Faithfull in
the '60s

BRENDAN, 25
OCCUPATION
artist/designer/
shop owner/
old soul
MY FASHION ICON
is Daniel Day-
Lewis in *Gangs
of New York*
THE BEST THING
ABOUT NEW YORK
is that it's not
L.A.: Death is
always around
the corner

MY
FAVORITE
PIECE OF
CLOTHING
is a
vintage
Run-DMC
adidas
sweatshirt
KAREN, 29

KATE, 25
OCCUPATION
writer
I'M WEARING
30-year-old
Italian boots
that belonged to
my mom
MY FAVORITE
PLACE TO SHOP
is my step-
mother's closet
MY FAVORITE PIECE
OF CLOTHING
is the Bernhard
Willhelm dress
that my boy-
friend gave me
THE BEST THING
ABOUT NEW YORK
is riding bikes
in heavy traffic

MY
FAVORITE
FASHION
TREND
is
warrior/
western/
blade-
runner
funk
KENYAN, 28

168

MY FASHION
ICON is
my grand-
mother—
she gets
every-
thing
made for
her in
Pakistan
BERRIN, 25

JOE, 20
OCCUPATION
student/band
member
I'VE BEEN
LISTENING TO
The Seeds, July,
Music Machine,
James Chance,
Horrors
MY FAVORITE
PIECE OF
CLOTHING is my
winkle pickers
MY FAVORITE
FASHION TREND
is '60s garage

DOMINICK, 30
OCCUPATION
DJ/booker
I'M WEARING
a camo jacket
designed by me,
hand-painted
patches, and a
deconstructed,
studded hoodie
influenced
by The Clash
MY FAVORITE
PLACE TO SHOP
is Beacon's Closet
in Williamsburg
MY FAVORITE
PIECE OF
CLOTHING is a
vintage suit I
bought in London
at the Portobel-
lo Road Market
MY FASHION ICON
is early Lemy
from Motörhead
with a little
bit of Bowie in
there

VALERY, 31
OCCUPATION
makeup artist
I'VE BEEN
LISTENING TO
Kasabian, Yo
La Tengo, Gogol
Bordello, Timmy
Schumacher,
Talking Heads
MY FAVORITE
PIECE OF
CLOTHING is
the leafy camo
hunting jacket I
bought from Wal-
Mart in Colorado
Springs
MY FASHION ICON
is my dog,
Gizmo, because
he doesn't wear
pants

DESIREE, 27
OCCUPATION
designer
I'M WEARING
a T-shirt and
a chain, both
from Greece and
both gifts, one
for me and one
for my roommate
MY FAVORITE
PLACES TO SHOP
are the Fulton
Mall and
Delancey Street
MY FASHION ICON
is Spencer
Sweeney

MY FAVORITE PIECE
OF CLOTHING is
a vintage floor-
length yellow
silk flapper gown
that makes me
look like a human
pineapple!

DARCY, 25

ELANA, 19
OCCUPATION
student/fashion
PR intern
I'M WEARING
a J.Crew pea
coat, American
Apparel leg-
gings, and
vintage boots
MY FASHION ICON
right now is
Rachel Bilson
THE BEST THINGS
ABOUT NEW YORK
is that you will
always see some-
one you know if
you want to, and
if not, everyone
just seems
to disappear

MY
FASHION
ICON
is
Alison
Gold-
frapp,
because
she's
seductive
ANNA, 20

SOPHIE, 24
OCCUPATION
designer
I'M WEARING
Levi's,
Mulberry,
vintage
I'VE BEEN
LISTENING TO
R&B—I'm a
secret fan!
MY FASHION ICON
is Kate Moss—
obvious, but
she's undeniably
stylish

THE BEST
THINGS
ABOUT NEW
YORK
are its
history
and its
people.
People are
not shy to
express
themselves
here
CHRIS, 25

<u>NOMI, 25</u>
OCCUPATION
singer/
songwriter/
producer
I'M WEARING THIS
'cause it's all
snug but not too
feminine
THE BEST THING
ABOUT NEW YORK
is the Spanish
food in
the ghettos

CHRIS, 27
I'M WEARING
something I
hate. If I had
my way, I'd have
on Dior Homme's
golden boots, a
threadbare 30-
year-old top,
and a coyote-fur
vest with lots
of silver chains
I'VE BEEN
LISTENING TO
Juliette and the
Licks, Hot Chip,
Elastica, Sheila
E, and Madonna
MY FAVORITE
FASHION TRENDS
are skinny
jeans and black
eyeliner
THE BEST THING
ABOUT NEW YORK
is the food
delivery
(I'm lazy)

ILIRJANA, 26
OCCUPATION
journalist/DJ
MY FAVORITE
PLACES TO SHOP
are secondhand
shops, I Heart,
Tsubi
I'VE BEEN
LISTENING TO
Kate Bush, Black
Strobe, Roxy
Music, Super-
pitcher, Pel Mel
MY FASHION ICONS
are Cosey Fanni
Tutti, Clara
Bow, and Vivi-
enne Westwood

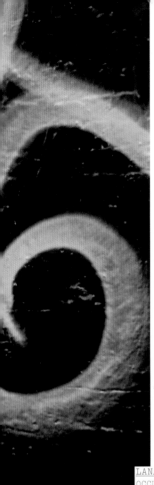

LANA, 29
OCCUPATION
stylist
I'M WEARING
Vest by Bar-
bara Bui that
I bought at
INA. Skirt is
from H&M. The
denim jacket is
by Judy Rosen
from the Good
the Bad and the
Ugly. Shoes by
Frederick's
of Hollywood.
I'VE BEEN
LISTENING TO
Cocteau Twins,
David Bowie,
Sigur Rós,
and Love
Psychedelico
MY FAVORITE
FASHION TREND
is the wedge
shoe because
they're comfy
and the extra
three inches
added to my legs
makes all the
difference
MY FASHION ICON
is my mother

place. It's a cutting-edge, creative, and underground hub of urban cool with an attraction that is more subtle than immediate, and which doesn't give itself up as easily as other cities.

While Bondi Beach and the Gold Coast in Sydney are veritable runways of surf style, Melbournians know there is far more to looking good than teaming the right sandals with a pair of board shorts. Here, the look is a more sophisticated mishmash of influences from East (Japanese quirkiness) and West (New York–style austerity and London-style punk), with a noticeably heavy dose of vintage. And if any store is a testament to Melbourne's eclectic style, it's Alice Euphemia on Swanston Street. Packed full of directional local labels including Obus and Life With Bird, it's also conveniently located right next door to perhaps the next best boutique in town, Genki, which features Australian labels such as Lover alongside a healthy amount of Japanese streetwear. Melbourne is also home to Toni Maticevski, arguably the

For too long Melbourne was known as Australia's second city, but it has finally emerged from Sydney's shadow to become the cultural—or perhaps countercultural—center of the Antipodes. Sure, Sydney may boast a superior location and 500,000 more inhabitants than Melbourne's four million, but Australia's most European city (more Greeks live in Melbourne than in any other metropolis apart from Athens) is also its most exciting. Buried in the architectural melting pot of Victorian Gothic and postmodern austerity are the best bars, clubs, boutiques, and restaurants in the country. There's no sparkling, photogenic harbor, no strangely shaped auditorium, but then Melbourne isn't a postcard kind of

SAM, 24
OCCUPATION
photographer
MY FAVORITE
PLACE TO SHOP
is Brunswick
Street

MEL.30

CAITLIN, 25
MY FAVORITE
PLACES TO SHOP
are Shag and
Curve
I'VE BEEN
LISTENING TO
Roisin Murphy
MY FAVORITE
PIECE OF
CLOTHING
is an early-
'70s ring
my mum handed
down to me

best high-fashion designer working in Australia, and the streetwear geniuses of Perks and Mini, whose eye-popping prints inspire slavish devotion among clued-in urbanites across the globe. But that elusive Europe-meets-the-Southern Hemisphere look is best achieved by paying a visit to Camberwell Markets, which cover an area the size of the Melbourne Cricket Ground (that's big, if you're not a cricket fan).

While the proliferation of boutiques, stately buildings, and trams rattling through the streets might occasionally be enough to make residents forget they're in Australia, Melbourne's nightlife puts the city in a league of its own. Whether you're winding up at the buzzing Prince of Wales club in cosmopolitan, seaside St. Kilda, or winding down at Revolver on Chapel Street (the best after-hours scene in the city), or the Mink Bar in the basement of the infamous Prince Hotel, the best time to spot the city's stylish denizens is after dark. And the hometown of AC/DC doesn't disappoint on the live-music front: The Ding Dong Lounge (sister to the Ding Dong Lounge in New York) and the Cherry Bar play host to the burgeoning local indie-rock scene, as do the more established Corner and Esplanade hotels.

Melbourne has long been called the most liveable city in the world, but it's also one of the most mysterious. Looking at these photos, you might not know where in the world they were taken; you might think you've spotted a London fashion student here, a Tokyo hipster there. But while Melbourne's position at the crossroads of world culture may make it a melting pot of style, the city is full of quirks that have to be experienced to be understood. It's a place that guards its secrets closely (one of them, by the way, is the Half Moon Bay in Brighton, which, with its phosphorescent plankton, is the best place on earth for a nighttime swim), but is all the more compelling for it.

(left)
SIVAAN, 20
OCCUPATION
waitress
MY FAVORITE
PLACE TO SHOP is
Hunter Gatherer
I'VE BEEN
LISTENING TO
Roots Manuva,
Elliot Smith,
Belle and
Sebastian, Fat
Freddie's Drop,
Lou Reed
MY FASHION ICON
is Johnny Vegas

(right)
JONNY, 20
OCCUPATION
customer service
MY FAVORITE
PLACE TO SHOP
is Retro Star
MY FASHION ICON
is Britney
Spears

LORELEI, 25
OCCUPATION
book editor/
musician
I'M WEARING
a tablecloth
MY FAVORITE
PIECE OF
CLOTHING is my
Octopussy dress
from Istanbul

AMY, 25
OCCUPATION
jewelry designer
I'M WEARING
dowdy clothes—
getting dressed
up is for single
people and job
interviews
MY FAVORITE
PLACE TO SHOP
is the garage at
my mum's house
MY FAVORITE
FASHION TREND
is aging men in
tight pants

MY FASHION ICON
is my father
TOM, 25

I'M WEARING
shorts so I can
cross my legs
when I sit down
ALLIE, 19

JOE, 23
OCCUPATION
designer/artist
MY FAVORITE
PLACE TO SHOP
is Retro Star
I'VE BEEN
LISTENING TO
Wolfmother, AC/
DC, Airbourne,
The Mess Hall,
Dallas Crane THE BEST THINGS
ABOUT MELBOURNE
are the food,
the music,
the people, and
the air

CLARE, 20
OCCUPATION
fashion student
I'VE BEEN
LISTENING TO
Tiger Army,
Youth Group,
Millionaire
MY FASHION ICONS
are my mum and
Josh Homme of
Queens of the
Stone Age
THE BEST THING
ABOUT MELBOURNE
is that you can
walk anywhere
in 45 minutes

THE BEST THING
ABOUT MELBOURNE
is that it is
as European
as you can get
in Australia

ANA, 19

EMMA, 30
OCCUPATION
shoe maker
I'M WEARING
a Rittenhouse
cardigan,
Beauty of Nature
dress, Princess
Tina leggings,
and sandals from
my own label,
Emma's Shoes
THE BEST THINGS
ABOUT MELBOURNE
are the shopping,
music, and bars

MATT, 23
OCCUPATION
musician
I'M WEARING
a flannel shirt
'cause I haven't
worn it in a
while and brown
shoes 'cause
they go well
with my flannel
shirt
MY FASHION ICON
is Shaggy
THE BEST THING
ABOUT MELBOURNE
is the weather

MY FAVORITE PIECE
OF CLOTHING is
a pair of Mexican
knitted socks
SUSANNAH, 24

TESS, 27
OCCUPATION who knows these days?
MY FAVORITE PLACES TO SHOP are Alice Eupehmia and Shag
I'M LISTENING TO Rick James, The New Electric, and Donovan
MY FASHION ICON is Warwick Capper and Joanne, his wife (behind every great mullet is a bigger mullet)
THE BEST THINGS ABOUT MELBOURNE are the weather and Parra by the Yarra

JENN, 26
OCCUPATION
actor
I'M WEARING this
for coverage and
comfort
I'VE BEEN
LISTENING TO
The Dears,
Black Heart
Procession, Smog,
and Johnny Cash
MY FAVORITE
PIECES OF
CLOTHING are
my rings that
I wear every
day-each one is
sentimental

ANDRE, 19
OCCUPATION
stylist
I'M WEARING
Tsubi jeans, D&G
glasses, Roy
V-neck, beat-up
Dunlops
MY FAVORITE
PLACES TO SHOP
are Alice
Euphemia and Fat
I'M LISTENING TO
Fischerspooner,
Black Eyed Peas,
Pedro the Lion,
Talk Show Boy
THE BEST THINGS
ABOUT MELBOURNE
are the local
bands and the
fashion scene

Tel: 9663 1223

JO, 36
OCCUPATION
artist
I'M WEARING
a vintage shirt
from Crown
Street in Syd-
ney, jeans from
H&M in Vienna,
and a utility
belt from Rus-
sell Street Army
Disposals

TOKYO

Paris and Milan may be the accepted global centers for fashion production, but Tokyo is far and away the world capital for fashion consumption. Nowhere else on Earth is a fancy wardrobe more widely and fiercely valued. Fashion is not just for the rich and snobby; there is a solid mainstream, middle-class embrace of designer goods and couture labels. For everyone from dainty office clerks to motorcycle-riding juvenile delinquents, identity starts and ends with a uniform; some are spontaneous creations, others are directed by widely read consumer magazines.

In the bubble economy of the mid-1980s, "fashion" very narrowly meant monochrome designer brands, and fourteen year-old kids dutifully stuffed themselves into pitch-black Yohji Yamamoto-style ensembles. By the end of that decade, however, teenagers got fed up, untucked their shirts, and rebelled against the authoritarian magazines. The media responded in the 1990s by creating a host of subcultural street fashion options: "mode," surfer, punk, mod, techno, hip-hop, and reggae for guys; and the wide spectrum of "Cutie," classy sorority-girl, icy high-fashion, deep-tanned and bleached-blonde "gyaru," and Gothic Lolita for girls. At the end of the decade, however, the borders between archetypes began to disintegrate,

and now the kids on the streets create a diverse bricolage made from an infinite number of international styles past and present. The days of Japan being imitative are long over, and now its citizens are recognized trendsetters in the realm of street fashion. We may single-handedly thank (or curse) the Japanese street scene and its international followers for the boom in limited-edition sneakers and hundred-dollar T-shirts. Tokyo has a huge number of shopping districts, each with its own distinct personality. Harajuku has always been Japan's main teenage fashion neighborhood, and on the weekends, kids come in from all over Japan to show off their version of Sunday best and buy new gear at their favorite stores, often waiting several hours in line to do so—many of the retailers sell the idea of exclusivity as successfully as they do clothing. Near the station, the infamous Gothic Lolita girls hang around in theatrical makeup and nineteenth-century European costumes. Behind The Gap is the hipster Ura-Harajuku region, housing A Bathing Ape, Head Porter, Real Mad Hectic, and all the other vintage-based streetwear lines emphasizing limited-edition products. From there, walking down Omotesando Road, one passes the European luxury brands' giant stores before hitting the "grown-up" fashion neighborhood of Aoyama, which features the warped blue-glass facade of Comme des Garçons' fantastical store and the towering new Prada building.

One train stop away from Aoyama and Harajuku, Shibuya is the sex and shopping district, home to the lumpen "ko-gyaru" high-school girls with bright-orange tans and hideous makeup, and their fashion mecca, Shibuya 109. Geographically close, but a world away, the neighborhood of Shimokitazawa has a less contrived, more punk-rock feel. Daikanyama, on the other hand, tries to be the Paris of Japan, with fashionable boutiques and cafés targeted mainly at more refined women in their twenties. A walk down the hill to the Nakameguro River finds shops with an eye to the graffiti culture of New York's Lower East Side, plus new trendy high-fashion stops like Frapbois.

The ongoing Japanese economic downturn has finally started to take a toll on the fashion market, but Tokyo still has a vitality and originality of street culture unlike any other city, East or West. And the best part is that no matter where you go within Tokyo, there is fashion insanity all around you.

KAZUTOSHI, 18
OCCUPATION
student
I'M WEARING
a Uniqlo jacket,
Device shirt,
and vintage
pants
I'VE BEEN
LISTENING TO
Hi-Standard, Mad
Capsule Market
MY FAVORITE PIECE
OF CLOTHING
is a rosary
MY FASHION ICONS
are Tadanobu
Asano, Masanobu
Andou, Joe
Odagiri

I'M WEARING
a punk look, but
I chose pink for
the skirt and
jacket so I don't
look too scary
SAILEN, 20

TAKAHIKO, 22
OCCUPATION
musician
I'M WEARING
whatever—there's
no concept
I'VE BEEN
LISTENING TO
Bodhi, Kyuss,
Velvet Revolver
MY FAVORITE
FASHION TREND
is the rock look

KAORI, 25
OCCUPATION office assistant
I'M WEARING the bohemian look—I want to dress like a celebrity
I'VE BEEN LISTENING TO Björk, Pushim, Moomin, Shonan
THE BEST THINGS ABOUT TOKYO are that it's busy and noisy, and everybody is selfish

KEN, 31
MY FAVORITE
PLACES TO SHOP
are Harajuku
and Shimoki-
tazawa
I'VE BEEN
LISTENING TO
The Vivians and
Test Icicles
THE BEST THING
ABOUT TOKYO
is that it's quiet

NAOKI, 20
OCCUPATION
student
I'M WEARING
a Martin
Andersson top
and Rad Musician
pants
I'VE BEEN
LISTENING TO
electro
MY FAVORITE
FASHION TREND
is simplicity

ERIKO, 20
I'M WEARING
coordinating
purple knits
MY FAVORITE
PLACES TO SHOP
are Koenji and
Harajuku
I'VE BEEN
LISTENING TO
Ska and Bossa
Nova
THE BEST THING
ABOUT TOKYO
is Asagaya

THE BEST
THING ABOUT
TOKYO is
Shimokitazawa
HIROSHI, 29

I'M WEARING pants
so tight my crotch
almost burst
SHINSAKU, 20

NORIKO, 22
OCCUPATION
student
I'M WEARING
a jacket I
made myself
I'VE BEEN
LISTENING TO
Utada, Avril
Lavigne, Björk
MY FAVORITE
PLACE TO SHOP IS
Shinjuku

MY FAVORITE
FASHION TREND is
rock style—but
not too crazy
RUI, 19

MOMO, 22
I'VE BEEN
LISTENING TO
Mary J. Blige,
Notorious B.I.G.
MY FASHION ICONS
are Rinka and
Kate Moss
THE BEST THING
ABOUT TOKYO
is that the rice
crackers are
famous

AYA, 21
OCCUPATION
student
MY FAVORITE
PLACE TO SHOP is
Shinjuku Isetan
THE BEST THING
ABOUT TOKYO
is that it's
calm and retro

YOSHIYUKI, 25
OCCUPATION
driver
MY FAVORITE
PLACES TO SHOP
are Shibuya,
Harajuku, Dai-
kanyama, and
Shimokitazawa
THE BEST THING
ABOUT TOKYO is
that the Tama
River is nearby

YOUICHI, 22
OCCUPATION
student
I'M WEARING
a denim jacket
printed with
logos of foreign
bands
I'VE BEEN
LISTENING TO
Mr. President,
Nirvana,
Slipknot
MY FASHION ICON
is Radiohead

227

MAKI, 22
OCCUPATION
student
I'M WEARING
some of my old
stuff, since
I've been
wearing the
same clothes
repeatedly
MY FAVORITE
FASHION TREND
is avant-garde

My favorite
fashion trend
is street
b-boy style
MASAHIRO, 20

TOMOKO, 29
OCCUPATION
accessory
designer
MY FAVORITE
PLACE TO SHOP
is Daikanyama
I'VE BEEN
LISTENING TO
the Beastie Boys
THE BEST THING
ABOUT TOKYO
is the café
around the cor-
ner from where
I live

MASARU, 24
I'M WEARING this
velvet tracksuit
because it's
comfortable and
cool and a bit
bad-boy-ish
MY FASHION ICONS
are the movie
Rockers and pho-
tographs from
Jamaica from the
'60s and '70s
MY FAVORITE
FASHION TREND
is the rude boy
look
THE BEST THING
ABOUT TOKYO
is that express
trains stop
at my station

MY FAVORITE
PLACES TO SHOP
are Harajuku
and Tokyo Bopper
RUMI, 24

YOUKO, 21
OCCUPATION
preschool teacher
MY FAVORITE
PLACES TO SHOP
are Shimokitazawa
and Kokubunji
MY FAVORITE
FASHION TREND
is lady-cute
MY FASHION ICON
is Kaede-San
THE BEST THINGS
ABOUT TOKYO
are the moun-
tains and the
kind people

IZUMI, 19
OCCUPATION
student
I'M WEARING
a skirt from
Tricot Comme des
Garçons
THE BEST THINGS
ABOUT TOKYO
are the many
people I meet-
young girls,
grandmas and
grandpas, cou-
ples, dogs. And
there are many
all-you-can eat
restaurants

GOU, 21
OCCUPATION
model
I'M WEARING
a textured
leather shirt.
It's my favorite
MY FAVORITE
PLACE TO SHOP
is Aoyama
I'VE BEEN
LISTENING TO
Jack Johnson and
Aimee Mann

AKIKO, 25
OCCUPATION
hair stylist
MY FAVORITE
PLACE TO SHOP
is Yokohama
I'VE BEEN
LISTENING TO
Benniek, Crys-
tal Kay, Misia,
Ketsumeishi
MY FASHION ICON
is You—that's
the name of
a Japanese
actress, not
you!

ITARU, 19
OCCUPATION
student
I'M WEARING
this because
I love Vivienne
Westwood
I'VE BEEN
LISTENING TO
Takuro Yoshida,
Rancid, The Sex
Pistols
MY FASHION ICON
is Johnny Rotten
MY FAVORITE
FASHION TREND
is London Punk

ASAMI, 21
OCCUPATION
hair stylist
I'M WEARING
something easy
and simple
THE BEST THING
ABOUT TOKYO is
the outskirts

ISAMU, 24
OCCUPATION
model
I'VE BEEN
LISTENING TO
Linkin Park,
Queen, Dr. Dre
MY FAVORITE
PLACE TO SHOP
is Beams

AZUMI, 21
OCCUPATION
hair stylist
MY FAVORITE
FASHION TREND
is black
MY FASHION ICONS
are people on
the street

THE BEST
THING ABOUT
TOKYO is
the retro
feeling
KASUMI, 22

SHUN, 22
OCCUPATION
designer
MY FAVORITE
PLACE TO SHOP
is Shibuya
THE BEST THINGS
ABOUT TOKYO
are the temples

SEIJI, 23
OCCUPATION
part-time worker
MY FAVORITE
PLACE TO SHOP
is in Osaka
MY FASHION ICON
is Harubou-San
THE BEST THING
ABOUT TOKYO
is nothing

I'M WEARING
green,
because
green makes
me feel
clean
NAOYA, 26

KAZUKI, 26
OCCUPATION
office worker
MY FAVORITE
PLACE TO SHOP
is Shimokitazawa
MY FAVORITE
FASHION TREND
is vintage
MY FASHION ICONS
are my friends

MY FAVORITE
PLACES TO
SHOP are
vintage
stores in
Daikanyama
YUKARI, 21

SHOPPING LIST

LONDON

TOPSHOP, topshop.co.uk
PORTOBELLO ROAD MARKET,
 portobelloroad.co.uk
PREEN AT CONCRETE 35a Marshall
 St., W1, +44 20 74344555;
 concretelondon.com
MIKI FUKAI mikifukai.com
EMMA COOK AT HARRODS, 87-135
 Brompton Road, Knightsbridge,
 +44 20 7730 1234
JONATHAN SAUNDERS
 saundersjonathan.com
BORA AKSU boraaksu.com
RICHARD NICOLL at Browns Focus,
 38-39 South Molton St., W1;
 +44 2075140063; brownsfashion.com
GILES DEACON AT SELFRIDGES,
 selfridges.com
VIVIENNE WESTWOOD 44 Conduit St.,
 W1R 9FB; viviennewestwood.com
MAHARISHI emaharishi.com
SILAS AT BOND, 17 Newburgh St., +44
 20 7437 0079; bondinternational.com
SPITALFIELDS MARKET SHERRIN ROAD
 (off Ruckholt Road), E10
CAROL CHRISTIAN POELL AT THE
 PINEAL EYE, 49 Broadwick St., W1,
 +44 20 7434 2567
MIU MIU 123 New Bond St., W1S 1EJ
 +44 20 73992030, miumiu.com
MISS SIXTY 39 Neal Street, WC2H 9PJ,
 +44 20 7836 3789; misssixty.com
BEYOND RETRO 110-112 Cheshire
 Street, E2 6EJ, +44 20 7-613-3636
BRICK LANE MARKET
 eastlondonmarkets.com
PRIMARK KINGS MALL, Kings Street,
 W6, +44 20 8748.7119
ROKIT 101 and 107 Brick Lane, E16SE,
 +44 20 7375 3864; rokit.co.uk
EUFORIA 61B Lancaster Road,
 +44 207 243 1808
CAMDEN STABLES Chalk Farm Road,
 Camden, NW1
CONVERSE converse.com
LEVI'S levi.com

COPENHAGEN

HENRIK VIBSKOV at Mads Nørgaard,
 Amagertorv 13-15, 1160 Kbh K, +45
 33 32 01 28; henrikvibskov.com
STINE GOYA stinegoya.com
WOOD WOOD Krystalgade 4, 1172 Kbh.
 K., +45 40 64 89 53
BAUM UND PFERDGARTEN Ryesgade 3F
 2200 Kbh. N, +45 35 35 21 15
ROCKWELL AT NORSE PROJECTS,
 Teglgaardsstræde 6a, Kbh. K,
 +45 33 93 26 26; norseprojects.com
DRIES VAN NOTEN driesvannoten.be
1206 Naboløs 3, 1206 Kbh. K.,

+45 33 73 12 06; 1206.dk
PEDE & STOFFER Klosterstræde 15,
 Kbh. K, +45 33 33 80 30
BEST BEHAVIOR Trepkasgade 9, Kbh.
 K., +45 35 24 72
PAUL SMITH AT A PAIR, Ny Østergade
 3, Kbh. K, +45 33 91 99 20; apair.dk
ACNE JEANS Gammel Mønt 10, Kbh. K,
 +45 33 93 93 28; acnejeans.com
HERMÈS Østergade 44, Kbh. K,
 +45 33 11 55 55; hermes.com
CHEAP MONDAY cheapmonday.se
HELLE MARDAHL hellemardahl.com
VIBE HARSLØF JEWELLERY at Pede &
 Stoffer
VANS vans.com
CONVERSE converse.com
NEW BALANCE AT WOOD WOOD
 Krystalgade 4, Kbh.K,
 +45 40648953; newbalance.com
ADIDAS AT WOOD WOOD
 Krystalgade 4, Kbh.K,
 +45 40648953
LACOSTE Ny Østergade 3, Kbh. K,
 +45 33 13 40 55; lacoste.com
STORM STORE Regnegade 1, Kbh. K,
 +45 33 93 00 14
LOLA PAGOLA Classensgade 4, Kbh. Ø,
 +45 35 42 66 00

BERLIN

BLESS Mulakstrasse 38, Mitte, +49
 30 275 96566; bless-service.de
APARTMENT Memhardstrasse 8 Mitte
 10178; apartmentberlin.de
ANDREAS MURKUDIS Münzstrasse 21/2
 courtyard (hidden) 10178,
 +49 30 30881945
COMME DES GARÇONS Karl-Marx allee
 78 10243 +49 30 28045338; gue-
 rilla-store.com
C-NEEON Konk, Raumerstrasse 36,
 10437; cneeon.de
MIROÏKE Strausberger Platz 19,
 10243; miroike.com
MARTIN MARGIELA Münzstrasse 21/2
 courtyard (hidden) 10178,
 +49 3030881945
PHRIEDJUNG phriedjung.de
BABY THE STARS SHINE BRIGHT
 babyssb.co.jp
LUCY BUKOVSKY Schönhauser
 Allee 156, Mitte
COSTUME NATIONAL
 costumenational.com
DSQUARED2 dsquared2.com
MIENTUS Wilmersdorferstrasse 73,
 10629, +49 30 3239077; mientus.com
EMERICA skatewarehouse.com
VANS vans.com
Y-3 adidas.com/y-3
ACNE JEANS Münzstrasse 23, 10178
 acnejeans.com

KLEIDERMARKT GARAGE, Ahornstraße
2, Schöneberg, +49 30 211 27 60
H&M Fritz-Lang-St., Mitte 12627 +49
30 99401870; hm.com

PARIS

LOUIS VUITTON 101 Avenue Champs-
Elysées; louisvuitton.com
VANESSA BRUNO 25 rue Saint-Sulpice,
75006; vanessabruno.fr
KITSUNE (by appointment only) rue
Therese, 75001, +33 1 42 60 34 28;
kitsune.fr
A.P.C. 112 rue Vieille du Temple,
75003, +33 1 42 78 18 02
CHARLES ANASTASE AT GALERIE
BAUMET SULTANA, 20 rue Sainte
Claude, 75003, +33 1 44 54 08 90;
galeriebaumetsultana.com
NICOLAS ANDREAS TARALIS,
26 rue St Gilles, 75003
MELODIE WOLF melodiewolf.free.fr
GUERRISOL 29-31, Avenue de Clichy,
75017
ZARA zara.com
AGNÈS B 2 Rue de Jour, 75001
REPETTO AT SHINE, 15 rue de Poitou,
75003; +33 1 48 05 80 10
GUCCI 27 rue du Faubourg-St-Honoré
75008
YVES SAINT LAURENT
43 Avenue Marceau 75016
DIOR HOMME 30 Avenue Montaigne
75008; +33 1 40735400
H&M 54 bd. Haussmann, 75009; hm.com
COLETTE 213 Rue St.-Honoré
SONIA RYKIEL 175, Boulevard St.
Germain, 75006, +33 1 49 54 60 60;
soniarykiel.com
ISABEL MARANT 16 Rue de Charonne,
75011; +33 1 4929 7155
ACNE at Colette
COMPTOIR DES COTTONIERS 59 Ter,
rue Bonaparte,75006
SPORTMAX AT MAXMARA, 31 Avenue
Montaigne, 75008
TOPSHOP at Colette
BALENCIAGA 10 Avenue George V,
75008 T: + 33 (0) 1 47 20 21 11
MARJAN PEJOSKI 48 rue Tiquetonne,
75002
HELMUT LANG 9 rue du Faubourg St.-
Honoré, 75008, +33 1 58625320
ZUCCA 8 rue saint roch — 75001, +33
1 44589888
ADIDAS 3 rue du Louvre 75001;
+33 1 42 60 34 83
COMME DES GARCONS 54 rue du Fau-
bourg St.-Honoré, 75008
XAVIER DELCOUR 3 rue d'Aboukir,
75002
CHLOÉ 54-56 rue du Faubourg St.-
Honoré and 44 Avenue Montaigne,
75008; chloe.com
CELINE 8 Ave Montaigne, 75008;
+33 1 49 52 12 01
ONWARD 147 Boulevard St. Germain,
75006; +33 1 55427756
PREEN AT SHINE, 15 rue de Poitou,
75003; +33 1 48 05 80 10
MANGO 6 boulevard des Capucines,
75009
MISS SIXTY rue Etienne Marcel,
75002
PRADA 5 rue Grenelle, 75006,
+33 1 45485314
ANN-SOFIE BACK annsofieback.com
RODEBJER rodebjer.com

NEW YORK

OPENING CEREMONY 35 Howard St.,
212.219.6988; openingceremony.us
BRENDAN DONNELLY 119 Ludlow St.;
brendandonnelly.net
PLASTIC PEOPLE plasticpeople.com
NOM DE GUERRE 640 Broadway,
212.253.2891; nomdeguerre.net
SURFACE 2 AIR 137 Grand St. Suite
402, 646.613.0097; surface2air.com
SUPREME 274 Lafayette St.,
212.966.7799
DARYL K 21 Bond St., 212.529.8790;
darylk.com
NARNIA 161 Rivington St.,
212.979.0661
TSUBI 219C Mulberry St.,
212.334.4690
DO KHAM 51 Prince St.,
212.966.2404
ALEX GAINES alexgaines.com
MADE HER THINK 227 Mulberry St.,
212.925.3890
ELEVEN 11 Prince St., 212.219.1033
MARC JACOBS 163 Mercer St.,
212.343.1490; marcjacobs.com
BEACON'S CLOSET 88 N.11th St.,
Brooklyn; beaconscloset.com
J. CREW 99 Prince St., 212.66.2739;
jcrew.com
AMERICAN APPAREL
americanapparel.net
BERNHARD WILLHELM AT SEVEN,
110 Mercer St. 646.654.0156;
sevenewyork.com
FULTON MALL Fulton St., Brooklyn
Levi's 536 Broadway, 646.613.1847;
levi.com
MULBERRY mulberry.com
I HEART 262 Mott St., 212.219.9265
INA 101 Thompson St., 212.941.4757
inanyc.com
H&M hm.com
THECAST
119 Ludlow St.; thecast.com
FREDERICK'S OF HOLLYWOOD
fredericks.com

MELBOURNE

ALICE EUPHEMIA shop 6, Cathedral
    Arcade 37 Swanston St.
OBUS AT FAT 52, 209 Brunswick St,
    Fitzroy, +61 3 94860391
LIFE WITH BIRD lifewithbird.com.au
GENKI shop 5, Cathedral arcade,
    +61 3 9650 6366
TONI MATICEVSKI AT FIGURE 8,
    +61 3 9650 2157
LOVER loverthelabel.com
PERKS AND MINI AT SOMEDAY, Level
    3, 252 Swanston St.; +61 3 6546458
CAMBERWELL MARKET
    sundaymarket.com.au
SHAG 130 Chapel St, +61 3 95108817
CURVE 158 Gertrude St, Fitzroy,
    +61 3 8415 1363
HUNTER GATHERER
    huntergatherer.com.au
RETRO STAR 37 Swanston St.;
    +61 3 9663 1223
RITTENHOUSE rittenhouse.com.au
PRINCESS TINA AT DOUGLAS & HOPE,
    80 Johnston St, Fitzroy 3065,
    +61 3 94170662 douglasandhope.com
TSUBI at Fat 5
DUNLOP FOOTWEAR
    dunlopsportsonline.com
RUSSELL STREET ARMY DISPOSALS
    aussiedisposals.com.au

TOKYO

A BATHING APE bape.com
HEAD PORTER 3-21-112 Jingumae,
    Shibuya-Ku, 150-0001,
    +81 3 57712621
REAL MAD HECTIC 4-26-21 protect bf
    Jingumae shibuya-ku,
    +81 3 3405 6933
COMME DES GARÇONS 5-3 minami-
    aoyama, shibuya-ku, 107-0062,
    81 3 57747800 Shibuya 109
FRAPBOIS A building 19-5 saru-
    gakucho shibuya-ku, 150-0033,
    +81 3 54592625
UNIQLO uniqlo.com
DEVICE 6-16-6 jingumae shibuya ku,
    150-0001, +81 3 57745107;
    device-kyoto.com
JEANASIS jeanasis.jp
E HYPHEN ehyphen.jp
MARTIN ANDERSSON
    martinandersson.co.uk
TOKYO BOPPER +81 3 3497 5528
ISETAN 3-14-1 shinjuku-ku,
    +81 3 3352111; isetan.co.jp
BEAMS 3-25-15 jingumae, shibuya-ku,
    +81 3 34703948
FALINE 1-7-5 jingumae, shibuya-ku,
    150-0001, +81 3 34038050

WEBSITES

Go to:

NYLONSTREETSTYLE.COM

for more pictures
and information
about this book.

Also check out:

NYLONMAG.COM

for more fashion,
art, music, beauty
and style news.

More street style
and photo websites:

thecobrasnake.com
lastnightsparty.com
teenageunicorn.com
epiclylaterd.com
tinyvices.com
style.com/peopleparties
ihatephotography.com
streetsrock.com
style-arena.jp/english/street/harajuku
torontostreetfashion.com
nypost.com/style/style.htm
gawker.com
ryanmcginley.com
electricafterparty.com
joshuawildman.blogspot.com
vertelife.com
isabelashapenzlien.com
staceymark.com
day19.com/jordan
jasonnocito.com
viceland.com